A Time To Speak Out

THE BIBLE, THE CHURCH, AND VICTIMS
OF DOMESTIC VIOLENCE AND ABUSE

ACKNOWLEDGEMENTS

The Directors and Members of Zion City Tabernacle

For their support

My wife, Sharon Queensborough

For knowing how obsessed I get with a

project and putting up with me anyway

The Lord Jesus Christ

For everything

A Time To Speak Out

THE BIBLE, THE CHURCH, AND VICTIMS OF
DOMESTIC VIOLENCE AND ABUSE

Windsor Queensborough

Published by

QB Sound and Print

A Time To Speak Out

The Bible, The Church, and Victims of

Domestic Violence and Abuse

Copyright © 2015 Windsor Queensborough.

All rights reserved.

ISBN 978-0-9935226-1-1

Author: Windsor Queensborough

Published by QB Sound and Print

www.qbsap.co.uk

No part of this book shall be reproduced or transmitted in any form or by any means, electronic or mechanical, including photocopying, recording, or by any information retrieval system without written permission of the publisher, except for the inclusion of brief quotations for the purpose of a review.

Also available electronically

Although every precaution has been taken in the preparation of this book, the publisher and author assume no responsibility for errors or omissions. Neither is any liability assumed for damages resulting from the use of this information contained herein.

CONTENTS

Page i	Foreword
Page iii	Preface
Page 1	Chapter One: Why Domestic Violence and Abuse?
Page 7	Chapter Two: Joseph's Story - Genesis 39:1-23
Page 11	Chapter Three: Joseph: A Survivor of Domestic Violence and Abuse
Page 15	Chapter Four: Below The Surface All Is Not What Is Seems
Page 23	Chapter Five: Getting Out
Page 33	Chapter Six: Hope For The Future
Page 37	Chapter Seven: Tamar's Story - 2 Samuel 13:1-20
Page 41	Chapter Eight:: Tamar: A Victim of Domestic Violence and Abuse
Page 45	Chapter Nine: The Humiliation Is Not Over
Page 51	Chapter Ten: A Family Conspiracy

Page 59	Chapter Eleven: The Desolation In Our House Must End
Page 63	Chapter Twelve: The Mindset of a Perpetrator
Page 73	Chapter Thirteen: Crimes, Forgiveness, and Reconciliation
Page 85	Chapter Fourteen: The Uniqueness of the Church
Page 93	Appendix One: A Response from Zion City Tabernacle
Page 97	Appendix Two: How the Church and Others Can Help
Page 101	Appendix Three: Useful Numbers (United Kingdom Only)
Page 103	More information: Not Another One About the Author

FOREWORD

In October 2015 our church hosted a conference entitled Not Another One: Putting A Stop To Domestic Violence And Abuse. Amongst other things we discussed in what way we were going to get the message out to a larger number of people. One of our presenters threw out a challenge: deliver it on a Sunday morning. Do it where we have a larger and captive audience. End the taboo around the issue and just confront it head on.

So we did.

The following Sunday our subject from the pulpit both morning and evening was Domestic Violence & Abuse in the Bible. I spoke from the stories of Joseph and of Tamar. This book is simply an extended version of the sermons delivered that day, along with added reflections.

Windsor Queensborough
Pastor, Zion City Tabernacle

PREFACE

I would not have been in a position to write this publication until now. The subject has long been taboo for many, including the Church, while a great many church leaders have been in denial - it doesn't happen in our church. I feel however that we are now in the midst of what I describe as a groundswell. It feels like there has very recently been a growing awareness of the subject of domestic violence and abuse and how the Church needs to respond. The demand for response is becoming more vociferous. More questions are being asked.

Besides our event in October I am aware of at least two gatherings in November with the intent to raise awareness and calling on the Church to be mobilised, and that was just within the black majority church. Of course it could just be me. You ever notice you never realised how many cars of a particular model were on the road until you bought yours? Events have doubtless been ongoing over many years but I still believe now is a significant time going into 2016.

This book is being written to awaken the ears and stir the voice of our churches. In opening our ears we are also releasing victims to speak. No more being hushed, no more struggling in secret, no more silent tears.

Chapter 1 describes how I was led to bring the subject to the attention of my church and subsequently beyond. Chapters 2 to 6, and 7 to 11 are devoted to two Bible characters: Joseph and Tamar respectively. Their stories reveal many of the issues surrounding domestic violence and abuse that are common with present day experiences. During these chapters we examine the challenges and thought processes of victims in an attempt to enlighten those on the outside who find such thought processes baffling, even contradictory. We also spend some time considering the tools of perpetrators and learning about manipulation and control. We also make it clear that we hold perpetrators 100% accountable for their actions.

In Chapters 10 and 11 particularly we start to raise questions of the Church, and the overall unwillingness or inadequacy to properly grasp this issue. Some of it makes for uncomfortable reading but it does begin to address the shifting attitudes that are necessary.

In Chapter 12 we take a more focused look at perpetrators. What drives them, what conceptions provide the foundation for abusive behaviour. We also challenge incorrect interpretations of scripture. Chapter 13 continues a scriptural focus as we address three key themes. Chapter 14 highlights the uniqueness of the Church to be in a position to do what I believe no one else can do: spiritual restoration. The Appendices present information about Zion City Tabernacle's approach to the subject, as well as insight from a former victim on how churches can make a positive impact.

It is my hope that this publication can be an encouragement and channel of inspiration to both victims and churches alike. I pray for each one of us to find our voice. If we can do this, lives are going to be transformed.

CHAPTER ONE:
WHY DOMESTIC VIOLENCE AND ABUSE?

Early in 2015 I was considering our church, and in particular our role as the people of God. In other words, our mission. Trying not to just come up with something for the sake of it I started to reflect on the mission of Jesus Christ himself since we are in fact his body on the earth. I know of course that there are many statements that Jesus made that inform us of his purpose for coming

I am come that they might have life (St John 10:10)

The Son of Man is come to seek and to save them that are lost (St Luke 19:10)

However I felt particularly directed to a statement Jesus made as recorded in the Gospel of Luke. On this occasion he went to his local synagogue as he usually did on the Sabbath. Jesus was given the honour of reading from the scriptures, and read from Isaiah. In chapter 4 Luke records his words as follows

The Spirit of the Lord is upon me, because he hath anointed me to preach the gospel to the poor; he hath sent me to heal the brokenhearted, to preach deliverance to the captives, and recovering of sight to the blind, to set at liberty them that are bruised, To preach the acceptable year of the Lord (St Luke 4:18,19)

This passage of scripture is very familiar to me, but somehow it made a specific connection with me this time around. I taught on it, we ran workshops on it. It was weeks later though that a particular line from the passage started to resonate with me in a special way

To set at liberty them that are bruised

I have always liked to make a comparison between that statement and one earlier in the same verse:-

To preach deliverance to the captives

These statements tell me that there are some people who simply need to be told that they are free. Nothing actually holds them captive except maybe the lack of information. Like some episodes of the crime dramas I watch all they need to hear from the investigators are the words "you are free to go".

Yet there are those who need more than a liberation message. These are held by shackles, either physical, emotional, spiritual. No amount of words on their own can be enough; some work, some activity is needed along with the words. In those episodes the words "you are free to go" are not enough – someone has to unlock the cell door!

Then I was drawn again to the words

them that are bruised

and immediately I made a connection with those who suffer domestic violence and began to consider their plight.

Some bruises are physical. They are the result of violent impact on the flesh. Though often accidental, those that concern us on these pages are quite deliberate. It does not matter how often a perpetrator claims they didn't mean it, these bruises are the result of a wrong choice.

Some bruises are emotional. Just like physical bruises they may not immediately appear. However given time the tell-tale signs will be there. But unlike physical bruises the pain lingers long after the initial impact. Physical bruises can look ugly for weeks even though the pain has gone. Emotional bruises may not show, but the pain can last a lifetime.

In that same week I received the latest monthly email from a church leadership group I subscribe to. The main theme that particular month delivered to me that very week? Domestic Violence. And then the following Sunday I happened to get into a conversation with a sister who had been attending our church for a while but whom I did not know very well. We got talking and during conversation she told me that she had written a book. When asked she told me the title "Not Bitter But Better", about her personal experiences of life, including domestic violence and abuse.

That was the final piece of confirmation I needed to let me know God was leading me towards this aspect of ministry. He directed us to take up the challenge of raising awareness

Why Domestic Violence and Abuse?

of this subject, one that is often considered taboo by many, especially within the church.

And here we are. Later I will outline what our church has done so far. But for now please follow me into the scriptures to find out what God thinks about the matter. Let us familiarise ourselves with the stories of two victims of abuse at the hands of family. Let us consider what part any or all of us can play in the mission of the Church, the mission of Christ - to set at liberty them that are bruised

CHAPTER TWO:
JOSEPH'S STORY
GENESIS 39:1 - 23

---

olours, and child by whoredom. And Ju'-dah said,
, This have and let her be burnt.
 coat or no. 25 When she was brought forth, she sent to her father
n's coat; an in law, saying, By the man, whose these are, am I with
is without child: and she said, Discern, I pray thee, whose are
 these, the signet, and bracelets, and staff.
 sackcloth 26 And Ju'-dah acknowledged them, and said, She
any days. hath been more righteous than I; because that I gave
 rose up to her not to She'-lah my son. And he knew her again no
ed; and he more.
to my son 27 And it came to pass in the time of her travail, that,
 behold, twins were in her womb.
-gypt unto 28 And it came to pass, when she travailed, that the
captain of one put out his hand: and the midwife took and bound
 upon his hand a scarlet thread, saying, This came out
at Ju'-dah first.
rned in to 29 And it came to pass, as he drew back his hand,
i'-rah. that, behold, his brother came out: and she said, How
ertain Ca'- hast thou broken forth? this breach be upon thee:
 took her, therefore his name was called Pha'-rez.
 30 And afterward came out his brother, that had the
he called scarlet thread upon his hand: and his name was called
 Za'-rah.

n; and she **39** And Jo'-seph was brought down to E-gypt; and
 Pot'-i-phar, an officer of Pha'-raoh, captain of
 son; and the guard, an E-gyp'-tian, bought him of the hand of
zib, when the Ish'-me-el-ites, which had brought him down
 thither.
rn, whose 2 And the LORD was with Jo'-seph, and he was a
 prosperous man; and he was in the house of his master
ed in the the E-gyp'-tian.
 3 And his master saw that the LORD was with him,
unto thy and that the LORD made all that he did to prosper in
ed to thy his hand.

1 And Joseph was brought down to Egypt; and Potiphar, an officer of Pharaoh, captain of the guard, an Egyptian, bought him of the hands of the Ishmeelites, which had brought him down thither.

2 And the LORD was with Joseph, and he was a prosperous man; and he was in the house of his master the Egyptian.

3 And his master saw that the LORD was with him, and that the LORD made all that he did to prosper in his hand.

4 And Joseph found grace in his sight, and he served him: and he made him overseer over his house, and all that he had he put into his hand.

5 And it came to pass from the time that he had made him overseer in his house, and over all that he had, that the LORD blessed the Egyptian's house for Joseph's sake; and the blessing of the LORD was upon all that he had in the house, and in the field.

6 And he left all that he had in Joseph's hand; and he knew not ought he had, save the bread which he did eat. And Joseph was a goodly person, and well favoured.

7 And it came to pass after these things, that his master's wife cast her eyes upon Joseph; and she said, Lie with me.

8 But he refused, and said unto his master's wife, Behold, my master wotteth not what is with me in the house, and he hath committed all that he hath to my hand;

Joseph's Story

9 There is none greater in this house than I; neither hath he kept back any thing from me but thee, because thou art his wife: how then can I do this great wickedness, and sin against God?

10 And it came to pass, as she spake to Joseph day by day, that he hearkened not unto her, to lie by her, or to be with her.

11 And it came to pass about this time, that Joseph went into the house to do his business; and there was none of the men of the house there within.

12 And she caught him by his garment, saying, Lie with me: and he left his garment in her hand, and fled, and got him out.

13 And it came to pass, when she saw that he had left his garment in her hand, and was fled forth,

14 That she called unto the men of her house, and spake unto them, saying, See, he hath brought in an Hebrew unto us to mock us; he came in unto me to lie with me, and I cried with a loud voice:

15 And it came to pass, when he heard that I lifted up my voice and cried, that he left his garment with me, and fled, and got him out.

16 And she laid up his garment by her, until his lord came home.

17 And she spake unto him according to these words, saying, The Hebrew servant, which thou hast brought unto us, came in unto me to mock me:

18 And it came to pass, as I lifted up my voice and cried, that he left his garment with me, and fled out.

19 And it came to pass, when his master heard the words of his wife, which she spake unto him, saying, After this manner did thy servant to me; that his wrath was kindled.

20 And Joseph's master took him, and put him into the prison, a place where the king's prisoners were bound: and he was there in the prison.

21 But the LORD was with Joseph, and shewed him mercy, and gave him favour in the sight of the keeper of the prison.

22 And the keeper of the prison committed to Joseph's hand all the prisoners that were in the prison; and whatsoever they did there, he was the doer of it.

23 The keeper of the prison looked not to any thing that was under his hand; because the LORD was with him, and that which he did, the LORD made it to prosper.

CHAPTER THREE:
JOSEPH - A SURVIVOR OF DOMESTIC VIOLENCE AND ABUSE

Many of us are familiar with the story of Joseph, the eleventh son of Jacob. If we were looking for a modern day word to describe his life the word 'rollercoaster' comes to mind. It is amazing to witness the various highs and lows that make up Joseph's life journey.

For those who are unfamiliar, Joseph was his father's favourite son, which he demonstrated by giving Joseph a special coat of many colours. He also sees the favour of God on his life and is gifted with the ability to dream of and interpret future events.

When it comes to his brothers however Joseph's favour has run out. They hate him for his position as favourite son, as well as his apparent habit of being a snitch. His brothers finally plan to murder him but end up faking his death instead and throwing him into a pit. They make sure that they destroy his multi-coloured coat. Later they get the opportunity to sell him to slave traders, who in turn sell him to Potiphar, a high ranking official in the Egyptian Pharaoh's palace.

The episode coming up now with Potiphar's wife is regularly viewed as a failed attempt at seduction. But closer inspection reveals that the story carries many of the hallmarks that we can readily identify as connected with domestic abuse. Firstly, despite Joseph's position as a servant, he is considered as part of the household, similar to family. Years earlier his grandfather Abraham while talking to God indicated that a son that was born to his servant could legitimately be considered as his heir (Gen 15:2,3). This places our story into a domestic household setting.

Favour once again is evident in Joseph's life and it seems it is not long before he rises to such a position where Potiphar entrusts him with running the entire household. Not only that but one bible translation states that he was "well built and good looking". How much more can one person have! Something about Joseph attracts the eye of Potiphar's wife and she makes a play for him.

Joseph has what seems to be a fantastic opportunity, the kind many young men would dream of. A chance of satisfying physical urges, which for the average twenty four year is like....well you know what that's like! A chance to satisfy emotional needs. Who doesn't like to be admired? And who doesn't like to feel wanted? A chance to taste forbidden fruit. Forbidden fruit has a way of inflaming sexual desire and heightening sexual tension. It seems the more you are told you can't have it, the more your flesh wants it. As Proverbs 9: 7 states

Stolen waters are sweet, and bread eaten in secret is pleasant

Everything for Joseph is on a plate. However Joseph is not like everyone else. He maintains a God-centered view. He is completely aware of all the favour he has experienced in Potiphar's house, and the trust that goes with it. A dream opportunity, the subject of many a man's fantasy, is turned down by this fit, well built, good looking young man.

For all of Joseph's attributes and for all his loyalty towards his master, the reason for rejecting this opportunity is that his focus is centred on his God:

How can I do this and sin against God?

CHAPTER FOUR:
BELOW THE SURFACE ALL IS NOT WHAT IT SEEMS

Joseph. Young. Successful. Well built. Good looking. Clearly a young man that is highly favoured. Who wouldn't want to be with him? Can anyone really blame Madame Potiphar for trying it on? How incredible would she feel with her body wrapped around this prize young stud?

When we think of the story it is not hard perhaps to picture Madame Potiphar simply as a lonely bored housewife. Being married to a successful husband can sometimes carry its own burden. What if his success means he is hardly at home? Or when he does come home he barely has time for her? Maybe he talks at her but actually pays no attention to her. A good career man is not necessarily a good husband. Who knows if he doesn't feel more affinity with his men than with his wife? It happens. Then into her home comes this young handsome foreigner. This sounds like the plot straight out of a dozen soap operas.

So what links this story with domestic abuse? What makes this anything more than a narrative of unrequited love?

Firstly Madame Potiphar makes a play for Joseph. She wants to jump his bones. The attention Joseph receives is perhaps initially flattering. But this continues daily. Every day she tries to seduce him and every day he refuses. But she refuses to take no for an answer. In short she is sexually harassing Joseph. What may have seemed flattering at first then soon becomes wearying, irritating, even depressing.

Below The Surface All Is Not What It Seems

Then consider that Madame Potiphar is doing this from a position of authority over Joseph. In his reply to her unwanted advances he states that Potiphar has put him over everything that he has except her. She continually attempts to exercise control and manipulate him into her bed. The pressure on Joseph continues until a day comes when all the rest of the other servants are out of the house. She makes an offer in a close up situation, close enough to grab hold of his clothes.

An ulterior motive

The remarkable thing is there is actually no indication that Madame Potiphar really had a thing for Joseph. Rather, the scripture text describes her as a devious manipulative woman with an agenda. Let's look closely again at her words recorded in verse 14, and one line in particular:-

See he hath brought in an Hebrew unto us to mock us

"He" who? Her husband Potiphar, that's who! Her first reference is not to the alleged actions of Joseph. No, her anger is directed primarily at her husband. For whatever reason, maybe the reasons alluded to earlier or maybe for some other unknown reason, she resents Potiphar and she uses Joseph as a pawn to strike back at him. Joseph is almost incidental.

Notice if you will who is the perpetrator and who is the victim. Stereotypical roles have been reversed, turning Joseph into the victim and Madame Potiphar into the perpetrator. Statistics tell us not only that 1 in 4 women suffer, but also that 1 in 6 men are likely to be victims of domestic violence and abuse during their lifetime.

What if we knew more of the reasons for her attitude? What if there was some dark secret from her past that has embittered her? Can we excuse her behavior? Can we make allowances for her abuse?

No.

No matter what may or may not have happened to her in her past, and no matter what may have been happening in her life at the time, Madame Potiphar has no excuse for abusing Joseph. All perpetrators need to know that domestic abuse is an individual choice without excuse.

It's not your fault

Victims especially need to know that there is no excuse for domestic violence and abuse. They need to know that they as victims are not at fault, not to blame for a perpetrator's actions. And yet many do just that. They look for reasons to justify a partner's behavior. They may even blame themselves. Was it something they did? Or failed to do? It can be hard for an outsider to understand. But psychologically many victims become imprisoned by their abuser. Searching for answers as to why this is happening to them, blaming themselves is a way to attempt to rationalise the abuse that they suffer.

Domestic violence and abuse is about manipulation and control. Abuse is often categorized into various types: Physical, Emotional, Psychological, Financial, and Sexual.

Did Madame Potiphar ever touch Joseph? Or did she caress him, or accidentally brush his hand with hers? Did she pinch his cheeks? Perhaps smooth his hair back into place? Unlikely somehow, but the problem is our attention nearly always turns to the physical. We tend to forget about the words "and abuse".

What does abuse look like?

If Joseph is being propositioned for sex every single day then it is abuse. Try, put yourself in his shoes. Every morning Madame Potiphar is saying "Joseph let's have sex". Every evening it's the same thing "Joseph let's have sex". Sounds like a dream for some; for Joseph this is a nightmare.

'Sticks and stones may break my bones

But words can hurt me on their own'

Don't believe me?

"I don't know what I ever saw in you"

"You would be nothing without me"

"No one would look at you twice"

"You have really let yourself go"

"Can't you do anything right?"

"You don't turn me on anymore"

"You're useless"

"If you say anything, I will make sure you regret it"

"You should have been home fifteen minutes ago"

"I would never let you leave me"

"Are you thick or what?"

"You're spending too much time with your family"

"One day I'll be gone and then we'll see what happens"

"If you ever leave me I will kill myself."

"And I'll take the kids with me"

If you are repeatedly being told that you are stupid it is abuse. If you are being verbally threatened it is abuse. If you are being consistently ridiculed and insulted it is abuse. If you have no say in how you spend even your own money, it is abuse. If none of your phone calls, text messages or emails can be viewed in private it is abuse. Abuse is not always violent. It is however always violating. Don't wait until the first slap or the first punch. Talk to somebody.

If you are forced to participate in sexual acts without your consent it is abuse. Joseph is the victim of a form of sexual abuse. But notice how Madame Potiphar turns the tables on Joseph and makes herself the victim. A determined perpetrator is a skilled manipulator. She is believable. Who is going to take the word of a Hebrew slave over that of the wife of an Egyptian high ranking official? She is devious. Notice the way she alienates Joseph and attempts to bond with the other servants. She states her husband has allegedly brought in this Hebrew slave to mock 'us'. I wonder since when she had considered the servants and herself to be 'us'? The other servants may well have resented the promotion of this outsider to a position of authority over them. Now Madame Potiphar enlists their support by identifying herself along with the servants as those who have been mistreated.

Skilled perpetrators are believable and manipulative. They do not belong to one race, or class, or educational background. They do not belong to one gender. They can be any age. They may even portray themselves as victims. A true victim has much to contend with.

CHAPTER FIVE:
GETTING OUT

Joseph now has to make the same choice that many victims are required to make....do I stay or do I leave? For us on the outside the choice seems obvious. So obvious that often we have a way of blaming the victim. How often do we hear the question, or even ask it ourselves – why don't they just leave? Here's why.

The choice to stay and put up with the abuse or to leave and escape is often a perplexing and agonising choice. Especially considering that the victim's thought patterns have been messed with and they are now emotionally vulnerable. There are traps to negotiate.

Like Joseph some victims can be trapped financially. Those who have no independent sources of income, or whose finances are completely under the control of an abusive partner have to ask how they are going to survive. This is multiplied whenever there are children involved. If Joseph ran away how was he going to live? Where was he going to live? If a victim of domestic abuse decides to leave the security of their own home, where will they go? Who will lend a hand?

Like Joseph victims can be trapped psychologically. He has had good treatment at the hand of Potiphar - where can he go where he will be treated the same? Abusers are in the habit of telling victims that no one will ever look after them as well as the abuser. They highlight and even create dependency so that victims can see no real alternative.

Joseph also shares another trait with victims – he is alone. The most devious and manipulative abusers will isolate their victim from their family. Abusers will denigrate friends, or maybe they will decide how often the victim can contact their own family. In some instances they are purposely moved to distant locations to reinforce their isolation. Joseph was alone, and in a foreign land – how could he possibly survive?

We can also wonder if Joseph would not be drawn back to childhood memories. Remember that he has been brutalised before at the hands of those close to him. Why is it that these things keep happening to him? Is it somehow his fault? Often a victim's self-esteem has been shattered at the hands of others. They can end up blaming themselves, excusing their abusers. Sometimes we even see a victim go from one abusive relationship to another, and we conclude they must like it. No. They don't like it. But somewhere along the line they have been made to feel that they do not deserve better. They have come to crave love and attention, even when that 'love' is twisted and that 'attention' is destructive. Make no mistake – this is not the fault of the victim, it is the fault of the perpetrator.

Leaving isn't easy

Joseph makes the decision to leave his home. His story gives credence to the fact that the most dangerous time for a victim is at the point of separation. Whenever an abuser becomes aware that the victim is making plans to leave they can become enraged. How dare she think she can make it without me? How dare he tell anybody? Post separation is an equally dangerous time for many victims. The most determined perpetrators will use everything in their power to locate the whereabouts of an escaped victim, with potentially fatal consequences. They will appear believable. They will even appear remorseful, and keen to make amends. Unsuspecting bystanders may well provide the help to perpetrators seeking their victims that endangers life.

With all of this going on it's no wonder that some victims feel that they cannot leave. They do not need to be merely told they are free; they need to be set free. Sometimes a victim sees their only hope of survival as staying in the situation and trying to cope. Just keep on smiling. Don't let anyone know what is going on behind closed doors. Learn how to use makeup to cover those bruises. If the makeup fails then always have an excuse at the ready. And another one. And another one. Keep doing everything you are told to do and don't let anyone know or become suspicious. If you are good maybe the beatings will be less.

The sad plain truth about abuse is that it almost never decreases, it escalates. Unless a perpetrator has a genuine change of heart and actively seeks help the abusive situation is likely to continue, and worsen.

Children at risk

We need to also consider the impact on any children that may be witnesses to the abuse. Although there are no children connected to this story, it is still worth commenting here. Evidence shows that there can be a devastating impact on the lives of those children that are brought up within an abusive environment. Children can be victims even when the violence or abuse is not directly aimed at them. They do not even have to be in the same room to be affected.

Exposure to domestic violence or abuse can often lead to children displaying aggressive behaviour, directed towards other children and/or parents, or in extreme temper tantrums. Abuse can be linked to medical conditions, common ones being asthma and allergies. Mentally it can be linked with depression. This should not lead us to jump to premature conclusions that where we see these symptoms there must always be an environment of abuse. However we all need to become more aware of the potential risks. The idea of staying within an abusive relationship for the sake of the children is not the best option. Although the children may not be physically hurt, they are almost certainly being harmed.

So how can anyone know when a perpetrator genuinely seeks to change their ways? How can a victim be sure that the apparent remorse is not just another stage of the repeated deadly pattern?

```
       Abuse
   ↗         ↘
Tension      Remorse
   ↖         ↙
       Gifts
```

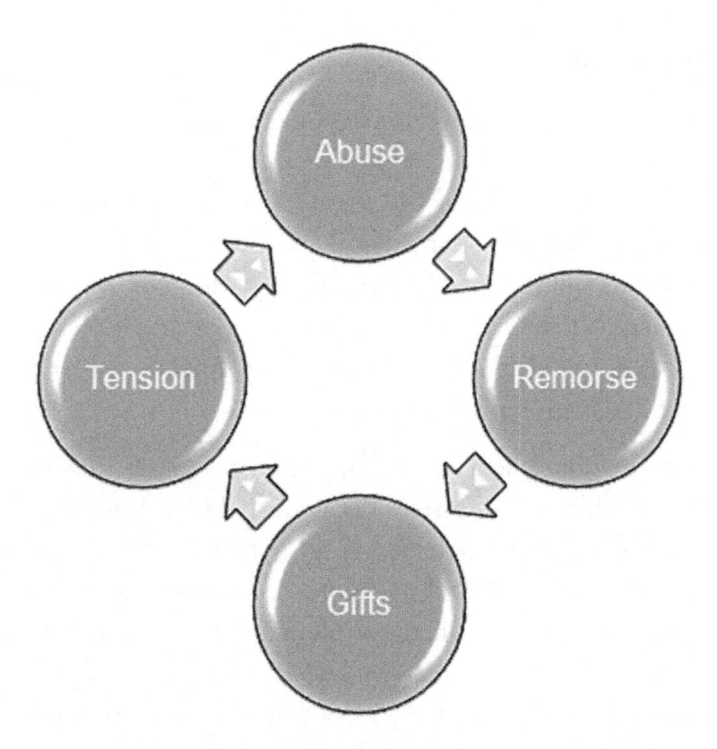

Abuse followed by Remorse followed by Gifts followed by Tension leading to Abuse...and so on

The subject is explored in more depth in a later chapter but the first pointer towards genuine change requires ownership. Perpetrators must admit that they are abusers. Such an admission must not be clouded with so called mitigating circumstances. If an abuser insists on blaming someone or something else for triggering what they perpetrate they are not taking ownership for their own actions. It is not the fault of the drink, or stress at work, or a negligent spouse. The blame always lies with the perpetrator. Working with perpetrators is not for the naively well intentioned. However, there is always hope that genuine change can take place.

A question of credibility

After leaving, Joseph then has to face another common problem for victims. Who is going to believe him? Who is going to take the word of a foreigner, a slave over that of the master's wife? Credibility is often bad enough for female victims, but can feel so much worse for male victims. Who is going to believe that she was coming onto Joseph and he turned her down? Which true red blooded male is going to pass up a chance like that?

Who is going to believe that a woman is beating up a man? What kind of man lets himself get beat up by a woman anyway? Who is going to believe that story? A recent experiment on television showed a male and a female actor acting out scenes of abuse in public. When the man was pretending to abuse the woman and dragged her into an alley, several bystanders came by to offer help. When the roles were reversed bystanders laughed.

Because of the fear of not being believed too many victims are silent. They will also not speak out for fear of being victimised even more. Some will not speak out because of shame. Others hold their peace because they believe their children will be safer that way. Sadly perpetrators are empowered by a victim's silence

Note: At this very moment as I sit here typing I am also half watching an episode of NCIS entitled Freedom (season 8, episode 13). A murder victim is found to have been a perpetrator of domestic violence on his wife, who like him was also a marine. No one around them had a clue of the repeated abuse that she had suffered, as the victim portrayed a strong character to the outside world and colleagues as a physical combat instructor. Apparently her silence was used by her to protect her persona – she was afraid to let anyone know that she of all people could possibly be a victim. Interesting!

Joseph, a victim of sexual abuse, ended up in prison for years. What a dilemma faces victims today. Escaping an abusive relationship is not the same as being free. When a woman is sitting in a refuge with her children amongst strangers in a strange location, even a refuge can feel like a prison. Getting out is only the first step towards freedom, but there is still a long process ahead. Physical freedom is but the first stage of liberty.

However the scripture declares

So if the Son sets you free you will be free indeed (St John :36) (ISV)

Getting Out

Free indeed! Let that be the vision for your life. Free indeed! Let that dream spur you on, encourage you, and empower you. The great civil rights leader Dr. Martin Luther King Jnr once declared at the end of his most famous speech those words that ring out "Free at last".

Jesus Christ, Saviour of the world, still declares to everyone who desires to be set at liberty,

"Free Indeed"!

CHAPTER SIX:
HOPE FOR THE FUTURE

Joseph has a long journey ahead of him, but it is a journey that ends with him on top. Despite the abusive treatment at the hands of perpetrators, despite being left to languish in the dark, his God-given skills come to the fore. He finally ends up being able to help others, he averts a national disaster, and creates an ongoing legacy.

Several times in his story, a certain truth is repeatedly established - the LORD was with Joseph. Whether he was in a pit, or a prison, or a palace, the LORD was with Joseph.

The scriptures declare that the Lord is with those who suffer domestic abuse

> *The LORD is close to the brokenhearted, and he delivers those whose spirit has been crushed (Psalms 34:18)*

May I take a moment to encourage someone to grab hold onto some truths? God has not abandoned us or forsaken us. He states in his word that wherever we are He will be also. Personally I hold that beyond physical location. I am persuaded that wherever I am in my life, emotionally, psychologically, He is with me. In all of my despair He is with me. In my darkness He is with me.

God has been thinking about us, making plans for us. He is not framing mischief against us, but has made provision for our peace. There remains hope for all of us for a better future. Our current situation is not our final destination.

Do not allow abusive treatment perpetrated by others to determine who you are, or what you can achieve. Every survivor was at one time a victim. Every victim has the potential to be a survivor. And even surviving is not the summit of what you may achieve. Joseph did more than survive. He made it to the palace. His dream, though it was seemingly delayed, did come to pass. I have sat in conferences and listened to stories of former victims who do more than survive, they now thrive. They are speaking out and helping to set other captives free. What was intended to destroy them has now become a means of breaking out other prisoners. The Lord is using them to blaze trails, to restore broken lives.

Your story is not over yet....

CHAPTER SEVEN:
TAMAR'S STORY
2 SAMUEL 13:1 – 20

CHAPTER 13

Amnon and Tamar

Now it was after this that Absalom the son of David had a beautiful sister whose name was Tamar, and Amnon the son of David loved her. 1 Chr. 3:9 • 2 Sam. 3:3

2 And Amnon was so frustrated because of his sister Tamar that he made himself ill, for she was a virgin, and it seemed hard to Amnon to do anything to her.

3 But Amnon had a friend whose name was Jonadab, the son of Shimeah, David's brother; and Jonadab was a very shrewd man.

4 And he said to him, "O son of the king, why are you so depressed morning after morning? Will you not tell me?" Then Amnon said to him, "I am in love with Tamar, the sister of my brother Absalom."

5 Jonadab then said to him, "Lie down on your bed and pretend

A Time To Speak Out

1 And it came to pass after this, that Absalom the son of David had a fair sister, whose name was Tamar; and Amnon the son of David loved her.

2 And Amnon was so vexed, that he fell sick for his sister Tamar; for she was a virgin; and Amnon thought it hard for him to do any thing to her.

3 But Amnon had a friend, whose name was Jonadab, the son of Shimeah David's brother: and Jonadab was a very subtil man.

4 And he said unto him, Why art thou, being the king's son, lean from day to day? wilt thou not tell me? And Amnon said unto him, I love Tamar, my brother Absalom's sister.

5 And Jonadab said unto him, Lay thee down on thy bed, and make thyself sick: and when thy father cometh to see thee, say unto him, I pray thee, let my sister Tamar come, and give me meat, and dress the meat in my sight, that I may see it, and eat it at her hand.

6 So Amnon lay down, and made himself sick: and when the king was come to see him, Amnon said unto the king, I pray thee, let Tamar my sister come, and make me a couple of cakes in my sight, that I may eat at her hand.

7 Then David sent home to Tamar, saying, Go now to thy brother Amnon's house, and dress him meat.

8 So Tamar went to her brother Amnon's house; and he was laid down. And she took flour, and kneaded it, and made cakes in his sight, and did bake the cakes.

9 And she took a pan, and poured them out before him; but he refused to eat. And Amnon said, Have out all men from me. And they went out every man from him.

10 And Amnon said unto Tamar, Bring the meat into the chamber, that I may eat of thine hand. And Tamar took the cakes which she had made, and brought them into the chamber to Amnon her brother.

11 And when she had brought them unto him to eat, he took hold of her, and said unto her, Come lie with me, my sister.

12 And she answered him, Nay, my brother, do not force me; for no such thing ought to be done in Israel: do not thou this folly.

13 And I, whither shall I cause my shame to go? and as for thee, thou shalt be as one of the fools in Israel. Now therefore, I pray thee, speak unto the king; for he will not withhold me from thee.

14 Howbeit he would not hearken unto her voice: but, being stronger than she, forced her, and lay with her.

15 Then Amnon hated her exceedingly; so that the hatred wherewith he hated her was greater than the love wherewith he had loved her. And Amnon said unto her, Arise, be gone.

16 And she said unto him, There is no cause: this evil in sending me away is greater than the other that thou didst unto me. But he would not hearken unto her.

17 Then he called his servant that ministered unto him, and said, Put now this woman out from me, and bolt the door after her.

18 And she had a garment of divers colours upon her: for with such robes were the king's daughters that were virgins apparelled. Then his servant brought her out, and bolted the door after her.

19 And Tamar put ashes on her head, and rent her garment of divers colours that was on her, and laid her hand on her head, and went on crying.

20 And Absalom her brother said unto her, Hath Amnon thy brother been with thee? but hold now thy peace, my sister: he is thy brother; regard not this thing. So Tamar remained desolate in her brother Absalom's house.

CHAPTER EIGHT:
TAMAR - A VICTIM OF DOMESTIC VIOLENCE AND ABUSE

The story of the rape of Tamar is a cruel heartbreaking one. Every rape is. Added to this, the fact that she is raped by her family is all the more deplorable. Where of all places should a girl find safety if not amongst family members? Amongst whom should a girl feel protected, if not in the presence of her own brothers? And yet in Tamar's story, her protection and security now become her abusers.

Kudakwashe Nyakudya, a survivor of domestic violence and abuse and founder of Kahrmel Wellness, describes two different types of domestic violence and abuse. Kuda describes Type 1 abuse as perpetrated by a single abuser. Type 2 is described as being perpetrated by a family or a community. Type 2 abuse includes instances of honour based violence (HBV) and female genital mutilation (FGM). At one time these may have been viewed as being unique to particular communities, but now the increase in inter-racial relationships means the impact may well be more widespread than first anticipated.

Let me say it again and make it clear: it is my view that Tamar was raped by her family. No, not just by a single family member, but raped by her family. The scripture also reveals a family conspiracy that goes further than you first think.

In our story we are presented with Amnon. A young man who has pent up sexual desires for his half-sister. His feelings are of such an intensity that he has become physically ill. The only thing that is preventing him from pursuing her is the fact that she is a virgin.

The lesson says Amnon had a "friend". Some friend. Jonadab was actually the son of David's brother, so a cousin. Amnon confides his feelings to Jonadab. Who knows if Jonadab could not have been able to talk him down? Instead he became an enabler. He uses his subtlety to devise a plan that Amnon executes all too well. He schemes to find himself alone with Tamar, after dismissing the escorts that were duty bound to be her chaperones. Amnon then overpowers his sister, and rapes her. None of Tamar's protestations could dissuade Amnon from his evil design. She vainly appeals to her dignity, and to his wisdom. She even offers to be joined to him in marriage by the consent of their father David.

Would she really have been prepared to marry a man who is ready to violently rape her? Some observers suggest she made this offer merely as a desperate last ditch attempt to escape. Alas her pleas fail. In a lust-crazed frenzy Amnon rapes his virgin sister, his last inhibitions finally overcome by his unholy desires. She tries to fight him off. The text says "being stronger than her, he forced her". Tamar did not willingly comply. She tried appealing to him. She fought to physically resist him. But all to no avail. She was forcibly raped.

Sex is a gift from God, designed as the highest physical expression of love between a man and a woman within a committed and sanctified relationship. It is such a powerful thing that God has imbued that same act with the ability to bring forth life. It is to be treasured and enjoyed by consent. So treasured is this act that the Bible advises against spouses withholding sex from each other, unless it is for an agreed period of devotion to God. However that gives no license whatsoever for sex to be forced on another, even within marriage. It is so hard to believe that as recently as 1991 rape within marriage was not recognized by UK law.

I wonder what Tamar had been imagining for the day that she would finally be given to a man. What were the dreams of a princess? What were her hopes, her plans? What would it be like to be held by a man for the first time? To feel those strong muscular arms around hers. Would she have been nervous, and tense? Or maybe she would be excited, alive? Maybe she would be all of those, and more. Whatever dreams Tamar may have nursed as a youth were shattered when she was cruelly violated. But it was about to get worse

CHAPTER NINE:
THE HUMILIATION IS NOT OVER

The King James translation says Amnon loved Tamar, but true love had nothing to do with Amnon's feelings. He was not in love, he was in lust. This is so vividly demonstrated by his subsequent treatment of her after he has raped her. Using devious manipulation and physical control he robs her of her virginity and dignity, and then callously dismisses her. His hatred of her exceeds the lust he had to have her. He treats her as a disposable object, with less respect than for a used condom. He has her thrown out of the house and makes his servant bolt the door after her. His action actually makes it appear as if it was Tamar who has tried to seduce him! Picture a once beautiful, now broken Tamar, lying in a crumpled heap on the floor outside the door. And then she hears the door being bolted behind her.

An unexpected reaction

It is Tamar's reaction to Amnon's hatred of her that adds a twist to this already heartbreaking story. She wants to stay. She begs Amnon not to dismiss her, calling this latest act worse than the actual rape. Worse? It is hard to imagine anything worse than the rape of a virgin by her brother. It is a paradigm that seems beyond belief, one which we as observers may struggle to reconcile.

But Tamar is now thinking of the utter shame that this will bring on her life. She is now thinking of what society will make of her as a victim of sexual abuse. No, they will not be sympathetic. No, they will not be consoling, or comforting. Society is about to victimise her again. She has been raped by Amnon and Jonadab. She is about to be violated again, this time by society.

No one will want her. Once a royal chaste princess the object of adoration, she will now become an object of derision. If she ventures out she will be the subject of bystanders' whispers. People will stare, and then when they catch her eye they will suddenly avert their gaze. Some will wonder whether she brought it upon herself. Maybe she led her brother on? Was she being provocative, a tease? Could she not have fought back or escaped? Did she even try? Why would a prince of Israel force himself upon his sister when he could presumably have the pick of all the beautiful virgins within Israel?

In Tamar's estimation her shame is worse than her rape. Amnon's rejection of her is worse than his brutality towards her. Where is her mind at, that she would even remotely consider staying with her abuser? I daresay her mind is possibly at the same place as the minds of many victims of domestic violence and abuse. How often do we ask the question "why doesn't she just leave"? In our own way we may well be inflicting more shame on a brutalised soul. We may well be making our own judgements based on ignorant assumption. As a whole we have not taken time to try to understand the mindset, the emotional turmoil and anguish of an abuse victim. From our safety we judge what she ought to have done, what we would have done if it happened to us. Unwittingly we are violating the victim again.

Why don't they just leave?

So, why is it that some victims choose to stay? Some perhaps are afraid of being alone. In their minds a toxic relationship is still better than no relationship at all. He might not be perfect, she may have her 'issues'; at least the person is there.

Some are afraid of the consequences. As I have said before, what will people say? How will I be treated if I am on my own? Victims can be trapped financially, having no visible means to be able to make their own way. Others are trapped by fear of trying to escape, just in case something worse happens. A fear of what will happen if the children become involved.

From the outside the solution seems clear to us. But we are dealing with victims who are emotionally abused. These are people capable in some instances of holding down high-powered positions at their place of work. Educated, empowered, envied by all. But behind that smiling face lays brokenness, hurt, shame. Behind that front door all the fears resurface, memories of a punch, the continuous stream of demeaning insults, and the steady erosion of identity.

The Humiliation Is Not Yet Over

So why won't victims of domestic violence and abuse report the abuser? Often the plain honest truth is many don't actually want to be separated from their partners. They still love them but they just want the abuse to stop. If they report their abuser there may well be no going back. It will be the final death knell of a relationship which in their view was not always bad. They cling on to what they deem as the good times, remembering better days. They magnify the abuser's good traits and diminish what they deem as momentary lapses.

"She is a great home maker".

"He would never hurt the children".

"She has had a harsh upbringing".

"He says he loves me".

"It was my fault, I just kept pushing".

"He always brings me flowers. Afterwards".

"He is so tender when we make up".

"They will change".

Again, the very sad reality is that unless a perpetrator sees themselves, takes ownership of their abusive actions, and has a genuine desire to change, the abuse will not simply go away.

It will escalate.

CHAPTER TEN:
A FAMILY CONSPIRACY

In my mind Tamar suffered from what has been described as type 2 DVA. It is my opinion that she was not raped only by Amnon. You also have to include Jonadab, a family member, as her rapist. Amnon had nurtured his lust for Tamar for no one knows how long. He was physically ill through his evil desires yet he never acted it out. That was until Jonadab his 'friend' showed up. What if Jonadab had talked him down, shown him the folly of his ways, or redirected Amnon who as prince could surely have had the pick of the nation? Why didn't he even warn King David of the darkness in Amnon's heart? Instead he used his wit to formulate an evil plan. He enabled Amnon, so he too must be classed as a rapist.

Tamar had a special garment of many colours, uniquely worn by royal princesses who were still virgins. It was not only a symbol of her privilege, but also a symbol of her honour. This garment signified her purity, her chasteness. After her brutal rape one of the actions Tamar performed in her degradation was to tear her special garment. Along with the other actions Tamar signaled her own humiliation. Amnon did not tear her garment; Tamar tore it herself. The violation was perpetrated by Amnon, enabled by Jonadab, but the judgement was pronounced on Tamar by Tamar herself.

So many more victims of sexual abuse have judged themselves. Many innocents have pronounced their own condemnations. Maybe it is a vain attempt at damage limitations? Is it that if victims condemn themselves they are hoping that others need not? Is it possible that they strip themselves before the baying mob, the jackals of judgement, have opportunity to further do so?

Together both Amnon and Jonadab raped Tamar. The family conspiracy however was still wider than the main two protagonists. It became clear that Absalom, Tamar's brother, knew there was an issue.

As soon as Absalom saw his sister he knew that something devastating had happened. The tearing of her garment of honour, along with the ashes and the wailing were a sure indication of what had befell her.

And Absalom her brother said unto her, Hath Amnon thy brother been with thee?

How did Absalom know to blame Amnon? He knew because he was already aware of Amnon's desire for Tamar. He immediately made the correct conclusion. No enquiry, no investigation needed. He just knew it. This indicates a family conspiracy. It must have been known that there was an issue. Maybe it was never openly spoken of, maybe never publically discussed, but family members knew all the same. Absalom knew that his sister was at danger of the lusts of their half-brother. The evidence suggests that he did nothing. No warnings for Tamar, no threats towards Amnon, no plea to their father David.

A time to speak out

There is a time to be silent, but there is a time to speak out. This was not the time for silence. Absalom had refused to speak out, and his silence conspired to rape his beautiful sister. And just like Absalom, too many families are silent. Too many churches have held their peace. We ought to have been shouting. We should have been raising the alarm. Instead we shouted about all the wrong things. We were not silent in our private phone calls where we shared the juiciest gossip. We were not silent when we broke people's confidentiality by turning private confessions into public sermons.

My fear is that many of our churches may well have unwittingly become conspirators in the domestic violence and abuse of our sisters, and our brothers. Not only have we been silent, we have silenced the victims. We too have assisted in the perpetration of domestic violence and abuse.

but hold now thy peace, my sister: he is thy brother;

Absalom sees his sister in her distressed state and he knows exactly what has happened to her. He also knows the identity of her abuser. What advice does he give to his beautiful but broken sister? Do not say anything, he is your brother. Never mind what you have suffered. Never mind that your life has been decimated. Never mind the fact that you have been betrayed by the very people who ought to have protected you. Just don't say anything. This is a family matter now; no one else needs to know. We do not want to bring down shame on the family name.

If you want to talk about shame let's talk about the shame of those families that have not merely stood by silently, but have actively offered their young ones over to the corrupt desires of older family members out of a warped picture of loyalty.

regard not this thing

Absalom tells Tamar to forget about it. Forget about your rape, and your subsequent humiliation. Forget too about your stolen virtue, your crushed aspirations, your dashed dreams. Pretend it never happened and move on. Sure, you will scrub your skin raw when you bathe but you will never feel clean. You will have times where you will break down without warning and sob uncontrollably. You will wake up screaming in the middle of the night. You may end up being alone for the rest of your life. People will whisper, people will point. The room will go silent when you walk in. Some will claim you wanted it. Others will say you deserved it because you thought you were better than everyone else. But he is your brother so let's not talk of it.

The failure of the Church

In what way have our churches hushed our victims, and become co-conspirators in their abuse?

"It's not our problem"

"Pray about it"

"It will bring shame on the church"

Church, it is our problem. When one bleeds, all bleed, when one cries all cry. Whoever hurts the body also offends God. This case does not require marital counselling. A crime has been committed within our midst.

Tamar has been raped and we say "pray about it". That advice is absolutely and completely useless. Yes, it is as useless as when James asks what's the point of telling a naked person "be warmed", or telling a hungry person "be filled" without handing them clothes or food *(James 2:15,16)*. We can decree and declare and cancel assignments and bind demons and break curses all we want. When we have done with making our grand power statements what are we going to do, I mean actually do, to back up our words? When are we going to put works to our professed faith?

We protect the shame of our church in order to preserve our public image. We do not want the church to be evil spoken of. Maybe it is not our evangelism we want to protect as much as to protect our fundraising! Decide now which is more shameful – a church that exposes offence or a church that victimises the abused. Which one do you think God is more concerned about – our image or His people?

A Family Conspiracy

So Tamar remained desolate in her brother Absalom's house

Tamar was left stunned, devastated by her ordeal, and remained so in her brother's house. What an indictment against Absalom. And what a judgement against the church whenever we allow our sisters, or our brothers, to be abused right in our midst, and then we muzzle them.

How many are still coming through our doors each week, singing and clapping, lifting hands and praising, listening to our sermons, and yet are still desolate?

How many are responding to altar calls and being prayed with and yet still carrying the hurt home with them?

How many have simply stopped coming, and maybe even stopped believing?

Exactly how did we allow the house of refuge to become the house of desolation?

CHAPTER ELEVEN:
THE DESOLATION IN OUR HOUSE MUST END

Joseph and Tamar. Two people both favoured, with bright futures ahead of them.

Joseph and Tamar. Two people who share the distinct privilege to wear significantly coloured coats.

Joseph and Tamar. Both of them victims of domestic violence and abuse. One ends their journey elevated to the palace. One starts from the palace and descends to a place of desolation. For every Joseph there is a Tamar. For every survivor there is a casualty.

As much as I celebrate Joseph, my eyes are stinging with tears for Tamar. There is a lump in my throat, and a knot in my stomach. Recently I was deeply moved at stories that I read on an online forum of those who were raped in the church. In the church. Their abusers were their 'christian' brothers. And what did the church do? The Church 'Absalomed' them. Hush child. Don't say anything. And try not to take it to heart. You will get over it. I know the Lord will make a way.

But times are changing and so is the Church. We are no longer closing our eyes, our ears, and certainly not our mouths. A generation has arisen that is saying no more desolation in the house of refuge. A generation is arising that says we are not afraid to take on the taboo subjects and the unspeakable issues.

What message does the church have for perpetrators? We will not harbour the spirit or attitude that promotes abuse. We will not allow or accept the manipulation and misinterpretation of scriptures to act as a shield for a perpetrator's abusive behavior. We will not be sending victims back to potentially life threatening relationships. We will support those who genuinely desire to change, but we will not do this in naivety. We are not ignorant of such devices.

A message for Tamar

What message does the church have for you, Tamar? What can we do to end your desolation?

We, the Church, will listen to you. We will not fob you off with clichéd scriptures. We are not embarrassed when you talk to us. We will allow you to talk, whether in confidence, or in conference. You choose how you wish to tell us, we will listen.

We, the Church, will believe you. It takes on average 35 incidents before a victim finally finds the courage to seek help and tell someone. You have overcome some incredible barriers just to find the strength to tell us. The last thing you need now is suspicion, accusation, and judgement.

We, the Church, will not hold you in bondage to abusive relationships. We will not put you under pressure to remain within harm's reach. We know that the same God who hates divorce also hates abuse.

We, the Church, will empower you to make choices. We will not tell you what to do. You have already had to contend with controlling relationships, we are not going to replace one with another. We will not insist that you leave or stay, but we will support you.

We, the Church, will educate ourselves about the help that is available to you and we will point you to that help. We will work with other agencies to provide for you. We will hold your hand through the processes that lay ahead of you. We will support you on your journey to liberty.

We, the Church will not merely proclaim your liberty, we will help set you free. We will bind up your broken heart and tend to your bruises. We will lift you out of the house of your desolation and restore you to your palace.

We, the Church, will be silent no longer. We will speak out on the issues that were once considered off limits. We will remove the gags which your abuser has used as a covering.

We, the Church, will empower all of our Tamars, and our Tamars shall become our Josephs.

Get ready Tamar. You are going back to the palace.

CHAPTER TWELVE:
THE MINDSET OF A PERPETRATOR

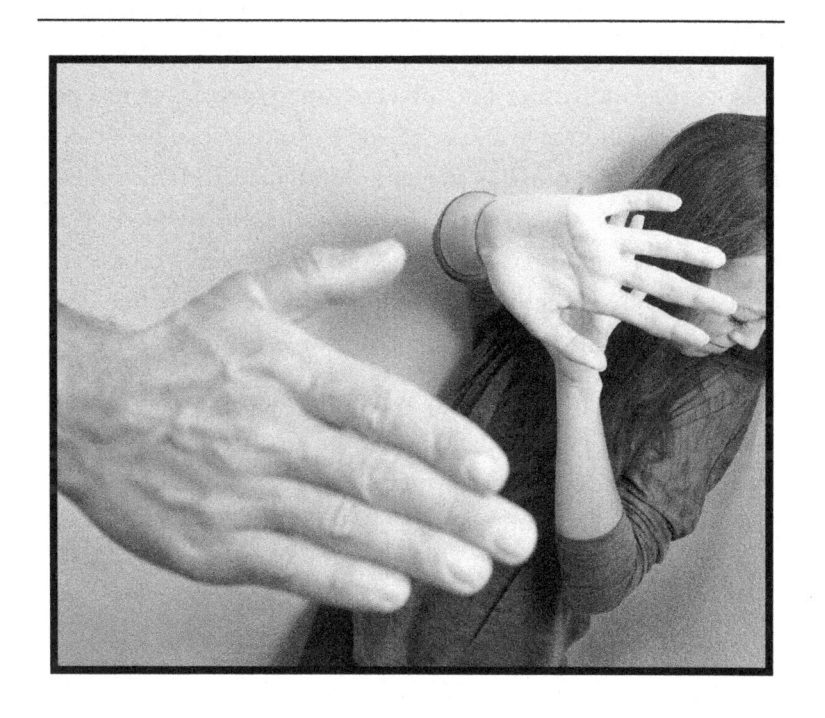

What makes one person abuse another within an intimate or family relationship? Throughout the previous chapters I have made it clear that the perpetrator is entirely to blame for abuse carried out towards another. No excuses have been offered to allow blame to be shifted. The act of abuse is deemed a choice.

It is naive however not to consider some of the factors that contribute to people making such poor decisions. One of my reasons for addressing the subject of perpetrators is to confront those who may be on the edge. No punches have been thrown - yet. No one has started to dominate and manipulate their partner or spouse - yet. Even Amnon, as messed up as he was, had boundaries that he would not initially cross. If I can just grab somebody's attention before those lines are crossed then a life, a family, may be spared from this hurt.

I want to examine just briefly what attitudes would tip someone over the edge, and what would turn a normal robust disagreement into a situation where one person seeks to completely control and oppress a loved one.

Self-Control

There is no doubt in my mind that some people are simply evil. No, I'm not clever enough to explain it. But what about that person who is on a slippery slope, desperately trying to cling on to what they know is right behaviour, but see themselves helplessly descending into the abyss. Let's be honest for a moment shall we. Who amongst us in a relationship has never become angry or frustrated? Which of us has never said harsh words in the heat of the moment which we have soon regretted? Very few I imagine.

He that hath no rule over his own spirit is like a city that is broken down, and without walls (Proverbs 25:28)

He that is slow to anger is better than the mighty, and he that ruleth his own spirit is better than he that taketh a city (Proverbs 16:32)

Temperance is an old fashioned word which simply represents the ability to control yourself. In a heated argument either party must in the middle of their frustration exercise self-control. Personal restraint is a must. Having said that it needs to be stressed again that domestic arguments are a far cry from domestic abuse. A simplistic difference is an argument is two way, abuse is one sided. In an argument each party may well give as good as they get. An abuse victim is not in a position to argue back. Continuously heated arguments are potentially damaging long term, an abusive relationship definitely is.

Growing up

Many people are affected by the environment that they have grown up in. A home where physical violence is the norm sends a message that this must be accepted and expected behaviour. A home where one partner literally rules with an iron fist has much potential to produce others of a similar disposition. Other forms of abuse can also set a pattern that needs to be broken. If you grow up seeing one parent abuse another emotionally, destroying confidence, belittling, dominating, it may be viewed by the impressionable as the 'norm'. Yet, there are many who have grown up within such unhealthy homes and have made a conscious pledge to themselves that they will never dish out that treatment towards another that they themselves have either witnessed or even experienced. So yes, abuse is still a choice, and a wrong choice too.

Expectations

Another factor in the treatment of one by another is expectation. Society itself has had a significant role to play in creating certain gender specific expectations, and these have contributed to values that when taken to extreme lengths produce abusive situations. A good example is sexuality.

When it comes to sex I wonder how many men were ever advised to "lie back and think of England". (Just as a side note I wonder, were other nationalities ever told to think of their particular country? But I digress). For years up until the Sexual Revolution it seems sex was done by men to women for men. It was a woman's duty to please her man. Such a one-sided view of sexuality did nothing to suggest equality. It helped to reduce a woman to a commodity, a piece of hardware.

Back in the day as we say the media was responsible for painting a more sinister picture, one that we never recognised at the time. Take almost any drama series or soap opera and you would inevitably encounter a scene where a man holds a woman in an embrace and kisses her. She struggles to break free and the man holds her more forcefully and kisses her again. The woman struggles but then mid kiss she gives in and willingly enjoins the passionate embrace. Familiar?

What did that teach us men? It taught us that if a woman says no she doesn't mean no. It means she is playing hard to get and wants to be forced. It seemed to say to men if you hold her tighter she'll change her mind. It said if you want to be a 'real' man you have to be prepared to play it rough. Imagine that attitude being promoted now. I am not blaming Hollywood and TV networks for rape. I am saying that societal norms may have played a significant part in framing faulty mindsets.

The 'roles' of men and women as applied from scripture and reinforced by society have created certain expectations. Woe betides our sisters when they fall short of our expectations. I never realised I held expectations of what I viewed as a woman's duty until I attended a training course entitled Tackling

Domestic Violence and Abuse in Faith Communities. One session addressed perpetrators' thought processes and particularly expectations, and in certain places quotes from the Bible were used. As I sat there listening I started to think of the way that I myself have quoted scriptures like that over the pulpit. It has made me rethink even some of the simple banter that I have previously engaged in.

When it has suited us we have selectively used the Bible to support our expectations regarding roles and responsibilities. So we insist that domestic chores are for women, and business and outdoor pursuits are for men. If our spouses dare step outside of our 'norms' we think it is our duty to slap or shame them back into place.

How narrow minded! The virtuous woman of Proverbs 31 could sew, knit, and cook, and was a proper little homemaker. She was also into property, market gardening, manufacturing and distribution, as well as import and export. She was kind hearted but she was also smart and physically fit, having good core and upper body strength. Meanwhile the New Testament describes Paul as sewing tents, and Jesus making the breakfast.

The 'S' word

The misuse and incorrect application of biblical texts have certainly played their part in framing expectations that fortified the minds of potential abusers. This has affected both men and women. If I want to trigger a certain type of response in many Christian women I need only to utter the 'S' word. No not Sex. The other 'S' word. Got it ladies?

Wives submit yourselves unto your own husbands (Ephesians 5:22)

You can watch some of the sisters visibly bristle as soon as the word submission is mentioned. Then you hear the counter charge

"Well if husbands would love like Christ loved the Church we would have no problem submitting"

Actually I can't argue with that.

One of my colleagues in the ministry at our church said something that has stayed with me ever since he said it. Derrick Campbell said that the instruction for wives to submit should not be taken as an instruction for husbands to subjugate their wives. That simple statement has enhanced my understanding greatly. Submission is nothing like subjugation, they are worlds apart. Part of our faulty thinking has no doubt come from watching too much wrestling. I am not even talking about WWE, I am going back to the days of World of Sport on Saturday afternoons. One wrestler would lay a hold on another in such a way as they were forced to submit and end the contest. Dear friend, if a submission is forced it is not a submission.

An underdeveloped ego

And they did not receive him, because his face was as though he would go to Jerusalem. And when his disciples James and John saw this, they said, Lord, wilt thou that we command fire to come down from heaven, and consume them, even as Elias did? But he turned, and rebuked them, and said, Ye know not what manner of spirit ye are of (Luke 9:53-55)

A phrase I learned from another ministerial friend, Reverend David Shosanya, has resonated with me. The need to control another person in every detail may well be linked to a sense of inadequacy within the abuser. Personal validation only comes by being able to command someone else. Others will try to compensate by the acquisition of things. David described this to me as an underdeveloped ego.

Although not a domestic setting the reaction of James and John when Jesus was rejected by the Samaritans, and the response of Jesus himself has lessons applicable here. They sought permission to call down fire on the heads of the unbelieving village, to perpetrate violence on those who never met their expectations. Jesus responded by telling the brothers they did not know who they were.

Have perpetrators lost their sense of identity? Do they violate others because they are confused about who they are, and were created to be?

The Mindset Of A Perpetrator

No man yet ever hateth his own flesh, but nourisheth it and cherisheth it. (Ephesians 5:29)

The only man that I can remember in the New Testament that hurt his own flesh was the man who lived in a graveyard and was possessed. The Bible describes in more than one place how two become one. A man who hurts his wife also hurts himself. No 'man' ever does that. It would be easy to say that any man who hurts a woman is not a real man. I suggest that an abusive man does not know what it is to truly be a man. The image of manhood has become lost, and lies have taken its place.

Part of the reason for addressing the mind set of the perpetrators is preventative. There are enough warning signs within these pages to help a potential abuser to seek help, and change before lives are destroyed. For those who have crossed the line the road to rehabilitation for a perpetrator is a long and arduous one, man or woman. With patience and perseverance and help, underpinned by a genuine desire to change, it can be walked.

A last word: abusers who sincerely want to change, do not change to win someone back. They change for themselves because they know it is right.

CHAPTER THIRTEEN:
CRIMES, FORGIVENESS, AND RECONCILIATION

Crimes

Dare any of you, having a matter against another, go to law before the unjust, and not before the saints?

Do ye not know that the saints shall judge the world? and if the world shall be judged by you, are ye unworthy to judge the smallest matters?

Know ye not that we shall judge angels? how much more things that pertain to this life?

If then ye have judgments of things pertaining to this life, set them to judge who are least esteemed in the church.

I speak to your shame. Is it so, that there is not a wise man among you? no, not one that shall be able to judge between his brethren?

But brother goeth to law with brother, and that before the unbelievers.

Now therefore there is utterly a fault among you, because ye go to law one with another. Why do ye not rather take wrong? why do ye not rather suffer yourselves to be defrauded?

Nay, ye do wrong, and defraud, and that your brethren.

(1 Corinthians 6:1-8)

If someone from our church who has suffered domestic violence at the hands of another church member makes a decision to go to the police and make a formal report, I will offer the victim whatever support I can.

That statement appears to fly directly in the face of the Holy Scriptures. However in order to correctly interpret and apply this scripture I believe we must make a distinction between civil and criminal law. Civil law covers disputes between two or more parties. They are pursued by one party against another, as in a lawsuit. Criminal law covers infractions against the law of the land and is prosecuted by the Crown.

When I read and reflect upon the passage of scripture in 1 Corinthians chapter six I see a dispute between two church brethren being taken to law courts. Disputes like these ought to be able to be settled by the parties themselves, or failing that by the Church. However I do not believe this scripture precludes a Christian from going to the police to report a crime committed against them, even if that crime is committed by another Christian.

For those Christians and churches who insist that such issues must not be reported to the authorities I have to wonder: what do our safeguarding policies say? God forbid, but if an allegation of abuse against a child is made, or it comes to our attention that a child is being abused, is it really our intention to handle that matter internally? Really?

Have we learned nothing from the stories of child abuse perpetrated by members of the clergy? Those religious organisations that tried to cover up years of abuse committed by known offenders? Their answer often was to move them to another parish. Hey smart move. Let's give known perpetrators a fresh supply of victims. Let's hide their identity and give them the perfect cover to continue their hateful crime. I'm sorry, but I believe we need a better plan than that.

If we become aware of a domestic violence and abuse issue that has an impact on a child, we have a statutory obligation to make a disclosure. There will be times when our faith brings us into conflict with the laws of the land. But based on the distinction between civil and criminal law I do not believe this issue to be one of them.

Forgiveness

And forgive us our debts, as we forgive our debtors

For if ye forgive men their trespasses, your heavenly Father will also forgive you:

But if ye forgive not men their trespasses, neither will your Father forgive your trespasses (St Matthew 6:12,14,15)

The disciples of Jesus asked their Rabbi for lessons on how to pray. After all the points that Jesus referred to in his model prayer, he returned to one point after he said Amen – that of forgiveness. He then made forgiveness the fulcrum on which the scales of our receiving forgiveness and the Father receiving our prayers are delicately balanced. If we refuse to forgive others, we can not expect to receive forgiveness from our Heavenly Father.

Part of the healing process of anyone wronged is being able to forgive the offender. This is no less true for any victim of domestic violence and abuse. Forgiveness as such is about setting oneself free, and actually helps to take away the hold that someone's act may have had on a victim.

Unforgiveness is a constant reminder of the wrong committed, and perpetuates the hurt inflicted by an abuser. It has the same impact as a sting that is left within an insect wound. Even after said insect is gone the sting continues to pump venom into its victim, and has power to do more harm than the initial wound. The sting has got to be removed before healing can take place. Unforgiveness leads to bitterness which in turn eats away at the very soul of the unforgiving one. Forgiveness may not make the pain immediately disappear, but through it healing will come.

Of course forgiveness is a process that needs to be worked through. The well-known orator T.D. Jakes once said something along these lines: forgiveness can be likened to a large ocean going vessel in the sea. The command to steer a new course can be given in an instant, but the momentum of the vessel means it takes time for the direction to change.

When the disciples heard Jesus say that we are to forgive our offenders not seven times but seventy times seven in one day, their response was

Increase our faith (St Luke 17:5)

I do not recall the disciples asking for increased faith for healing the sick, or for casting out demons, or any other thing besides forgiving one who has offended them.

Forgiveness is an act of faith. You may not notice any immediate change and the pain may still be incredibly raw, but stand on the words of the Saviour. Believe that since he has commanded it, he has also provided you the capacity to carry it through.

By the way 'forgive and forget' is not a biblically based principle, at least not in the way the statement is used. Many people are held captive by the notion that if you remember the offence against you then you have not truly forgiven the offender. They incorrectly believe that to forget means to erase from memory. Joseph forgave his brothers but still remembered that it happened!

In the Bible to forget does not mean to 'remove from memory' - it means to 'remove from focus'. Paul made a list of the things that were associated with his former life, in which he used to trust for righteousness. Things such as 'circumcised the eighth day', and 'tribe of Benjamin'.

Then he says this

> *...this one thing I do, forgetting those things which are behind, and reaching forth unto those things which are before (Philippians 3:13)*

How could he say he has forgotten those things which are behind him when he has only just listed them out? Because the things behind him were still in his memory, but they were no longer in his focus. Do not nurture or feed your hurt, but neither should you feel condemned whenever you remember what has happened to you. You are still in the healing process. Rather focus your thoughts on future restoration.

Reconciliation

> *And all things are of God, who hath reconciled us to himself by Jesus Christ, and hath given to us the ministry of reconciliation (2 Corinthians 5:18)*

Having thus addressed the subject of Forgiveness it becomes necessary that we also turn our attention to the matter of Reconciliation. This issue is one of the most profound pillars of our lives as Christians. Yet it is also the single biggest challenge in matters of abusive relationships.

Reconciliation speaks to us of restored relationships. As God was in Christ, reconciling the world to himself, so now we as the Church have been given the mandate to preach the same message. However the Church can never truly preach about reconciliation to God without preaching reconciliation to each other.

Here then is a serious challenge: in matters of domestic violence and abuse how can we seek to reconcile a victim to their abuser? Can we send a woman back to be used as a punch bag by her abusive husband, or a man back to be assaulted by his wife? It would not surprise me to find that throughout history the Church has either naively or carelessly sent victims back to abusive partners, and in so doing have unwittingly jeopardised peoples' lives.

I believe that one myth that needs to be laid to rest is that reconciliation should be a direct consequence of forgiveness. I do not believe that to be correct. Rather I believe that true reconciliation can only be possible as a consequence of true repentance. Without repentance there is no right to reconciliation, even where the victim has forgiven the abuser.

Notice that Jesus hung on the cross and cried out:-

Father forgive them for they know not what they do (St Luke 23:34)

Fifty days later Peter told 'them' that they have crucified the Lord and Christ and that they need to repent (Acts 2:36-38). The fact that Jesus Christ has offered to us forgiveness does not automatically lead us to a right relationship with God - we have to repent to be reconciled.

Here is a serious note of caution. Not every perpetrator who says they are sorry *are* actually sorry. As has been said before, many perpetrators are skilled in the arts of manipulation and control. They can be adept at saying what the victim wants to hear, what the children want to hear, what other agencies want to hear. They have probably 'apologised' dozens of times to the victim, only to repeat the same destructive behaviour as before. This is many times worse when the victim has separated from the abuser, either by leaving or else by having the offending party removed. A scheming perpetrator will seek any means to be reunited with their victim in order to exact revenge for being exposed, or to regain control of their victim. They will employ any means in order to find an escaped victim's location, deceiving the best of us. It has been known for some perpetrators to attend programmes designed to address their behaviours, only for them to compare notes!

This is where I believe the Church is often particularly vulnerable. One of our most essential principles is that people can change, and we encourage and welcome people to do just that. It is one of the main reasons that the Church exists. Unfortunately this has led to victims feeling pressured into taking back their abusers. Call it naivety or call it negligence, we have ourselves at times been guilty of perpetrating domestic violence and abuse.

A Genuine Repentance

The question to be asked is how can the Church seek to protect vulnerable victims while at the same time carrying out the mandate of preaching for changed lives. How can we achieve this balance?

We must recognise true repentance, and there must be genuine evidence. That firstly means that an abuser must unequivocally accept 100% responsibility for their actions. There must be no resorting to blaming others or circumstances or environment or substances - no excuses whatsoever.

Secondly the abuser, if genuine, must also seek help to change. Repentance is much more than feeling sorry, or saying sorry. True repentance must lead to a change. I also believe it is best that such help should come from recognised professionals. The Church should certainly be involved but in truth I would not advocate leaving this work solely in the hands of unqualified people. Working with perpetrators is a skill.

Now I know this once again will fly in the face of those who hate the idea of the church looking towards outside help. However would you please consider for a moment the sad plight of someone who falls and breaks their leg at church.

Should we:-

1. pray
2. call an ambulance
3. pray while we call the ambulance

If our church was to suffer a burglary would we:-

1. pray for a spirit of conviction on the thief
2. call the police
3. pray for a spirit of conviction while we call the police

I think you see where I am going with this! I believe we are much better positioned if we make connections with other agencies. As long as we keep such organisations at a distance we are increasing their suspicion of us. It is far better that we voluntarily engage with them, and be prepared to learn from them as well as educate them.

We really need to educate ourselves in all matters of domestic violence and abuse. Without recognising the warning signs we are in danger of attempting to correct abusive relationships with regular marital counselling, with potentially disastrous results.

Finally please consider that on many occasions where a perpetrator is seeking help to change, they should be prepared to do so from outside of the family home. The victim must be allowed a safe space in which to recover. Contact between the parties will probably be prohibited or at least restricted during this period. A willingness to allow this is another indication of genuine repentance.

With all of the caution that I have just advised, the reality is that there are precious few programmes out there for perpetrators. If we would diligently set out to educate ourselves, combined with the knowledge of the power of God to transform people, then who is to say that the Church cannot become agents of real change?

We as the body of Christ have been given the 'ministry' and the 'word' of reconciliation. Just look at that for a moment. The 'ministry' and the 'word'. Not word only. The ministry of Jesus Christ was described in the book of Acts as what he:-

Began both to do and teach (Acts 1:1)

Our ministry is to bring Joseph and Tamar back to the image God has purposed for them from the beginning.

For both to be restored to the palace

CHAPTER FOURTEEN:
THE UNIQUENESS OF THE CHURCH

I have been very keen in previous chapters to stress the need for churches to engage with outside established agencies. I view this as necessary in order to be effective in helping victims to overcome the trauma of domestic violence and abuse. In an ideal situation we would have all the resources, skills, finances to be able to give a complete and holistic solution to those in need. The truth is that very few churches have those resources, those skills and that finance. If we wait until we do, we will lose many victims in the process.

No one else

Having said all of that, it is now vital to note that the Church is uniquely positioned to do what no one else can do, and that is to offer spiritual restoration to those who are broken. If we believe there is no other God but one then there is no other institution on the earth like the Church. There are many community groups, many social enterprises, many forums and many self-help groups. Together they often do tremendous good. There is however only one Church, one organisation that carries the presence of the True and Living God. There are things that the Church needs to bring to the picture to affect complete restoration. Much has been said about the mouth and the fists of the perpetrator. Now let us consider what the hands and the voice of the church will accomplish, and how.

We Must Remember

Victims of domestic violence and abuse must be remembered. By that I mean that they should not be pushed aside and forgotten about, the result of a tick box exercise. When you go back to the stories of Joseph and Tamar you will see each one has a significant two year period. Joseph asked for his fellow prisoner to remember him when he got out, only for the butler to forget about him for two years. For two years Joseph was left in prison, wondering if he would ever be remembered. True, he was successful within the prison system and once again rose to the top, nevertheless it was still prison. Absalom exacted revenge on Amnon after two years. Two years of plotting, calculating, waiting for the perfect opportunity for bloody vengeance. In that two years no word of Tamar comes to us. Nothing of her progress, nothing of a possible rehabilitation. As far as we know she remained desolate until she died, right there in her brother's house.

As a pastor of a church that is newly and actively pursuing ministry to those affected by matters of domestic violence and abuse, I am trying to achieve the right balance. I do not want to make this a hobby horse, but neither can I let it be subsumed amongst all the other calls for ministry and resources. This is where I am grateful for the support group that will be able to take issues forward, and above all be able to respond to the needs of people affected.

I wish to make a special mention of the Methodist Church and their initiative 'Domestic Abuse and the Methodist Church – Taking Action' It is a set of comprehensive guidelines on the subject that appears well thought out and resourced. However what counts is what happens off the paper.

A Time for Grief

Have you ever watched a loved one die, and felt powerless to help? I have. It was not long and drawn out, it was mere moments as I watched my mother suffer a heart attack right before us. I kept thinking to myself that I am a minister, surely I should be able to stop this. Surely I should have enough faith to pray and turn things around. Alas, I couldn't.

Many will testify that going through a divorce is akin to bereavement, as one mourns the death of a marriage. In that case going through a marriage or relationship ended through domestic violence and abuse must feel like being witness to a violent murder. I have tried to explain the many emotions that a victim goes through, emotions which even sometimes appear irrational to a bystander. A victim who comes out of an abusive relationship must be given space to grieve if they wish to grieve. Something once precious and treasured has died. No, it has been murdered.

I remember preaching at my brother's funeral a couple of years ago from the Beattitudes:

Blessed are they that mourn for they shall be comforted (St Matthew 5:4)

I said in my address that people often seem to read that verse as "blessed are the comforted". We want to rush to the comfort but we deny space to mourn. Sometimes the mourning is painful to watch, painful to hear. It is painful to see others in pain, and to feel a little helpless in the process. But give space. Give time. The comfort that we offer is most appreciated against a backdrop of mourning, just as light becomes most effective at night.

Much more than just a victim

We do a great disservice to sufferers of domestic violence and abuse when we hold them merely as victims. We render them as incapable and smother them with pity. The danger is that we once again assume control over their lives in determining when they will be able to recover, and become effective again. While we as the Church remember their trauma and pain let us also recall their gifting.

Remember Joseph. It took two years but eventually the butler remembered there was a man he knew in prison who had the ability to interpret dreams. No doubt Joseph would have remained incarcerated were it not for a crisis moment arising. The thing is, his abusive treatment never eradicated his dream, or his gift. If we are going to help victims to overcome we have to see them as more than what they have been through. Neither the victim nor the church should allow the shameful abusive behaviour of an individual or a community to become that which defines an individual. That individual was born for more than that.

One of my favourite passages of scripture is

> *Blessed be God, even the Father of our Lord Jesus Christ, the Father of mercies, and the God of all comfort; Who comforteth us in all our tribulation, that we may be able to comfort them which are in any trouble, by the comfort wherewith we ourselves are comforted of God (2 Corinthians 1:3,4)*

I love the poetic flow, but I love the meaning more. It states that we are able to comfort other people in trouble by the same comfort we received from the God of comfort. There are former victims of domestic violence and abuse that are now in a position to share their stories with others, and more so empower others to break free. They have had their personal experience of desolation, but thankfully that was a chapter in their lives, it was never meant to be the whole book. In one of the stories I heard the Church failed in its duty and it was left to the police to become her Good Samaritan. But past failings will not become the epitaph of the church. We may never repair the torn coats, but we can walk alongside victims on the journey back to the palace.

The Uniqueness Of The Church

What the Church can do that no one else can do is be an agent of spiritual restoration. Many former victims have turned their lives around and each one deserves to be applauded and celebrated. The journey finds its completeness when our spirits are restored back to a right relationship with our Heavenly Father. Even the most precious earthly relationship may fail, but I hold to His words spoken through the prophet

Can a woman forget her sucking child, that she should not have compassion on the son of her womb? yea, they may forget, yet will I not forget thee (Isaiah 49:15)

God has not forgotten, and neither will we.

Peace

APPENDIX ONE:

A RESPONSE FROM ZION CITY TABERNACLE

Who is Windsor Queensborough to speak on behalf of the Church?

Well no one really. So let me speak out on behalf of our congregation, Zion City Tabernacle. This is what our church has done so far.

Well over a year ago we invited Kudakwashe Nyakudya of Kahrmel Wellness to address our church on a Sunday evening on the subject of domestic violence and abuse. Her story was both enthralling and disturbing at the same time. Not everyone was ready to hear it but it laid a great foundation for us.

In July this year myself and Yvonne Brown, a sister from our church, attended a one day training session run by Kahrmel Wellness on Tackling Domestic Violence & Abuse In Faith Communities.

At the beginning of September I presented an overview at church on the subject, again on a Sunday evening. I described how tackling domestic violence and abuse was consistent with the mission of the Church, which in turn is the mission of Christ himself. At the same time I announced a conference to be held at our church to be entitled Not Another One: Putting a Stop to Domestic Violence and Abuse.

Weeks later we invited Carol Davies, a Safeguarding training consultant and an Independent Domestic Violence Advocate, to deliver training on Domestic Violence and Abuse and the Impact on Families to a small group of volunteers. We formulated a strategy to offer support to victims, and even perpetrators, primarily by acting as a signposting organisation.

We set up a support group formed of the volunteers and prepared a help card for them for instant information re telephone numbers for key agencies.

In October we held the conference as planned. We invited presentations from Kuda, Carol working along with Audrey Spence, a probation officer, Sergeant Tony Parker of West Midlands Police, renowned gospel singer and founder of the Woman to Woman Foundation Christine "Cie" Hamilton, and finally Joyce Rose author of Not Bitter But Better. We also provided information from women's shelter The Haven, in Wolverhampton.

We have drafted a policy on Domestic Violence and Abuse stating how we will assist victims who make confidential disclosures to us.

We have now placed a wealth of literature within our reception area, and have placed discreet information within our rest rooms.

A Response From Zion City Tabernacle

We have set up a confidential telephone line and email address, and have created a Facebook page which we will use from time to time to supply information and inspiration.

Our plans are to extend our education and skills through further training. We will be enlisting male volunteers. We will be seeking to establish working relationships with established professional agencies such as The Haven, and Wolverhampton Domestic Violence Forum, amongst others.

We, The Church known as Zion City Tabernacle, are committed to putting a stop to domestic violence and abuse.

APPENDIX TWO:
HOW THE CHURCH AND OTHERS CAN HELP

We asked author and survivor of domestic violence and abuse, Joyce Rose, how we can help victims to move on. Here is her response…

Requires genuine compassionate team or individuals that are particularly passionate about helping victims of DVA

Helpful to have a good understanding of the impact of DVA

Be non-judgmental

Allow the person to speak

Advice of the support available for them to make their own informed decision

Be understanding and empathetic that the person disclosing may not be able to articulate everything about how their feeling in words

Be spiritually sensitive of what is required

Pre marriage Christian counselling,

Pre baptism counselling,

New converts foundation teaching,

Host the anointing that breaks the yokes and lift heavy burdens, it's not enough for us to go through rituals

Be ready to switch on a flip i.e. been sensitive to the Holy Spirit, i.e. if you have a pre sermon be ready to put it aside for what God wants to do and say. You never know who comes into your congregation desperate… be able to discern…

Provide prayer and deliverance behind the scenes as well as upon request; have a prayer list that extends far further than brethren to brethren

Seek knowledge about the wider issues in our community; some of the common themes that we all hear and know about are honour killings, genital mutilation

Make time to be friendly to visitors that come into church and not bypass them because their face doesn't fit or because you don't know them.

Wear love and compassion as visitors are coming into our churches desperate for answers and solutions… unfortunately many have come and gone empty

There are little or no programmes for perpetrators of abuse; does the church or we as the 'saved ones' have the answer? Do we have the toolkit in the book?

Don't beat people up if you don't see them for every service as worship is a lifestyle not as something we do on a Sunday where we come and are prompted to worship….worship is what I do for Christ in my walking in my talking and how we live our lives with each other.

How The Church And Others Can Help

Remember the gospel is bigger than a Sunday sermon...it is through greater works; healing the sick...living in the overflow by-reaching the community... not how many times your light can blind minds!

Living/giving others the good news that there is hope, no matter what ethnicity, culture or gender... that Jesus Christ He is still in the healing business... He reached me when the church unfortunately wasn't ready

The church has an ongoing crucial part to play particularly in assisting emotional and spiritual healing

Don't be afraid of people who come from differing backgrounds whether it be a gang member, different religious or faith backgrounds, but stand strong in the foundations of the gospel that there is one God who came and sacrificed His life for all regardless of race or gender etc.

The church has the key to breaking down strongholds, doing it all with LOVE and compassion. For God so loved... That He gave. When one tastes the love of God personally and through the ministry of the church they will not be able to continue in abusive relationships - because a wonderful change will come over them that they will want more - losing the appetite for the old life.

Have a visible information wall/table that provides practical advice and information regarding support agencies.

Don't collude: be ready to make a safeguarding referral whether it be for adult or child - always let the person know where possible

Be equipped ready and willing to walk the journey of transition with that person.

Buy/rent refuges and accommodate those in need

Joyce Rose

APPENDIX THREE:
USEFUL NUMBERS (United Kingdom only)

Emergency 999

The Haven (24 hours) 08000 194 400

Police (non-emergency) 101

SAYA Multi Lingual helpline (Bengali, Gujarati, Hindu, Punjabi, and Urdu) 0800 389 6990 (24 hours)

Karma Nirvana (honour crimes and forced marriage helpline) 0800 5999247

Forced Marriage Unit 020 7008 0151

Broken Rainbow – LGBT 08452 60 44 60

National Domestic Violence Helpline 0808 2000 247

National Centre for Domestic Violence 0844 8044999

Men's Advice Line 0808 801 0327

Respect (for people who are abusive to partners) 0808 802 4040

THANK YOU

Thank you for reading my book. I really hope that it has been a worthy read, and that you have been both informed and inspired. Please go back to whichever retailer you bought it from and leave a review. What follows is more information about support work that we offer at Zion City Tabernacle in respect of domestic violence and abuse, and some background information about myself.

Thanks again!

Windsor

NOT ANOTHER ONE

Not Another One is a confidential non-emergency support service for anyone who is affected by domestic violence and abuse. If you would like to discuss anything on this subject please feel free to contact us as follows:

Message support line: 07 804 930 961 (UK only)

Email: naodva@gmail.com

Find us also on Facebook: Not Another One

www.facebook.com/notanotheronedva

Not Another One is a part of the ministry of

Zion City Tabernacle

126 Compton Road, Compton, Wolverhampton WV3 9QB

Telephone: 01902 712232

Email: zionct@hotmail.com

Website: www.zioncitytabernacle.org.uk

ABOUT THE AUTHOR

I am passionate about helping victims of domestic violence and abuse to overcome their trauma. I am equally passionate about the Church taking this subject seriously, and offering real help to those who come to us for refuge, as well as those right within our midst.

Our church was mentioned in The Voice Online after we organised a conference on the subject matter. I was subsequently invited to a workshop sponsored by the Pentecostal Credit Union, where I was able to connect with like-minded Christians who are equally passionate about helping victims to survive, and making the Church a safe place.

On Thursday 14th April 2016 I have been invited to participate in a unique national educational conference entitled:

Tackling Domestic Violence & Abuse in Faith Communities: A Focus On The Church.

Contact Kahrmel Wellness for more details. If you are near Nottingham that day maybe I can see some of you there.

I have served as the pastor of Zion City Tabernacle in Wolverhampton, West Midlands, since it started in November 2008. I am part of a wonderful ministry team and sometimes have to pinch myself when people who I respect call me their pastor!

My ministry gifts primarily encompass exhortation and teaching. I have had the privilege of sharing these throughout the U.K., North America, and the Caribbean over many years.

I have been happily married since 1986, and have three grown children. I also work as a civil servant.

Contact me via Facebook

Personal email via windsorq@hotmail.com

Check out also details for some of my colleagues:

Kudakwashe Nyakudya

Kahrmel Wellness CIC; www.kahrmelwellness.com

Carol Davis Consultancy & Training

NLP LifeSkills Coach; info@cdct.co.uk; www.cdct.co.uk

Christine 'Cie' Hamilton

Email address: ciehamilton@yahoo.co.uk

Joyce Rose

Author of Not Bitter But Better; ISBN 978 1 781483 21 3

A Time To Speak Out

For

Audrey, Carol, Corol, Georgina, Joyce,

Marion, Peaches, Susan, Verona, Yvonne

Jeff, Granville

Tajel, Raw – told you I would

Made in United States
North Haven, CT
25 September 2022